Hope Through the Ages

A Poetic Journey Through the Old Testament

Amy Michelle Rogers

WESTBOW
PRESS®
A DIVISION OF THOMAS NELSON
& ZONDERVAN

Copyright © 2017 Amy Michelle Rogers.

All rights reserved. No part of this book may be used or reproduced by any means, graphic, electronic, or mechanical, including photocopying, recording, taping or by any information storage retrieval system without the written permission of the author except in the case of brief quotations embodied in critical articles and reviews.

This book is a work of non-fiction. Unless otherwise noted, the author and the publisher make no explicit guarantees as to the accuracy of the information contained in this book and in some cases, names of people and places have been altered to protect their privacy.

Scriptures taken from the Holy Bible, New International Version®, NIV®. Copyright © 1973, 1978, 1984, 2011 by Biblica, Inc.™ Used by permission of Zondervan. All rights reserved worldwide. www.zondervan.com The "NIV" and "New International Version" are trademarks registered in the United States Patent and Trademark Office by Biblica, Inc.™

WestBow Press books may be ordered through booksellers or by contacting:

WestBow Press
A Division of Thomas Nelson & Zondervan
1663 Liberty Drive
Bloomington, IN 47403
www.westbowpress.com
1 (866) 928-1240

Because of the dynamic nature of the Internet, any web addresses or links contained in this book may have changed since publication and may no longer be valid. The views expressed in this work are solely those of the author and do not necessarily reflect the views of the publisher, and the publisher hereby disclaims any responsibility for them.

Any people depicted in stock imagery provided by Thinkstock are models, and such images are being used for illustrative purposes only. Certain stock imagery © Thinkstock.

ISBN: 978-1-9736-0903-2 (sc)
ISBN: 978-1-9736-0904-9 (hc)
ISBN: 978-1-9736-0902-5 (e)

Library of Congress Control Number: 2017918002

Print information available on the last page.

WestBow Press rev. date: 02/12/2018

To my family,

my extended family,
and church family.

I always thank my God for you because of His
grace given to you in Christ Jesus.
1 Corinthians 1:4

CONTENTS

Acknowledgments xi
Introduction xiii
Prologue xv

CHOSEN SEED 1
Genesis

PROFOUND CALLING 5
Exodus

BOOK OF LAW 7
Leviticus

BALAAM'S HEART 9
Numbers

MT. NEBO 11
Deuteronomy

MIRACLES AND MAJESTY 13
Joshua

FINISHING STRONG 15
Judges

THE HEART OF A SERVANT 17
Ruth

THE COVENANT OF THE LORD 19
1 Samuel

TRUSTING GOD 21
2 Samuel

SOFT WHISPERS 23
1 Kings

FAITH TO SEE 25
2 Kings

WHEN GOD ANSWERS NO 27
1 Chronicles

NO OTHER IDOLS 29
2 Chronicles

TRUE REPENTANCE 31
Ezra

LEADING THE PEOPLE 33
Nehemiah

COURAGE IN FAITH 37
Esther

HEAVEN WISE 41
Job

PURSUING GOD 43
Psalms

THE PATH 47
Proverbs

PURPOSED DAYS 49
Ecclesiastes

BLESSED UNION 51
Song of Songs

HOLY, HOLY, HOLY! 53
Isaiah

YAHWEH WILL LIFT UP 57
Jeremiah

THE LORD RESTORES 61
Lamentations

REBORN 63
Ezekiel

COURAGE DEFINED 65
Daniel

TURNING AROUND 69
Hosea

LOCUS CALLED 71
Joel

TRUE MEASURE 75
Amos

PRIDEFUL DECEIT 77
Obadiah

THE RELUCTANT PROPHET 79
Jonah

NO GRAY LINES 83
Micah

HE BECKONS 85
Nahum

LIVING FAITH 87
Habakkuk

HEART'S CONDITION 89
Zephaniah

YOUR TREASURE 91
Haggai

GOD'S LOVE LETTER 93
Zechariah

FIERCE LOVE 95
Malachi

Afterword 97
Abbreviations 99

ACKNOWLEDGMENTS

I would like to thank my dad, Dr. John M. Rogers, who is literally a genius (scoring above the 99th percentile on the SATs, as well as scoring in the top 3 percent of the top 1 percent in the Competition for National Merit contest). The only less-than-stellar mark he has ever received was in the poetry section of an English class because he didn't care for it. Knowing that piece of history makes your encouragement that much more meaningful!

I would like to thank my twin sister, Kathleen Ellen Carr, who has been my best friend since the womb. She is the author of the children's book *Smile with Me Forever and Ever, Even with ALS*. This book was written in dedication to our mom, Dr. Patricia J. Rogers.

I would like to thank my dear friends Dale and Beverly Barrett, who have been monumental in encouragement and affirmation along my journey.

INTRODUCTION

Hope through the Ages was written to inspire the reader to delve into the Old Testament books of the Bible with an enlightened perspective. Intimacy with God is woven through the pages of this book, bringing connection to the stories of old in practical ways and offering encouragement in faith.

This book will take you on a poetic journey through the Old Testament, walking alongside the people, prophets, and books before Christ. *Hope through the Ages* is just that, a collection of poetry told in a way that brings personal connection to the Old Testament. This book invites you to read it as a daily devotional or to read it alongside your own personal journey through the Old Testament.

Each step of faith brings us closer to God and the hope of what is to come. This collection of poetry shows that God is ever-present in His unfailing love with His touch of grace and mercy, bringing life to every believer who comes to Him. The heart of this poetry is meant to deepen the relational understanding of the one, true, eternal God.

May His face shine upon you as you continue on your journey to learn and grow in God's amazing love.

PROLOGUE

The journey begins with Adam and Eve at the start of creation in Genesis and takes the reader through the hills and valleys of Israel's people and its prophets' relationship with God. The book concludes with a love letter written by God in Zechariah and a display of God's fierce love in the concluding chapter of Malachi.

CHOSEN SEED
Genesis

"The angel of The Lord called to Abraham from heaven a second time and said, 'I swear by Myself, declares The Lord, that because you have done this and not withheld your son, your only son, I will surely bless you and make your descendants as numerous as the as the stars in the sky and as the sand on the seashore. Your descendants will take possession of the cities of their enemies, and through your offspring all nations on earth will be blessed, because you have obeyed me" (Genesis 22:15–18).

In the beginning, God created.
From the empty, dark, and desolated,
He spoke and said, "Let there be light,"[1]
And out of the darkness, there was light.
He painted the blue in the sky and sea
And formed the mountains, hills and trees.
Every creature, great and small,
Our sovereign God made them all.
He created the heavens and the earth,
Forming a place for the nation's birth.
Out of the dust,
His likeness entrust
The day He formed Adam and Eve.
Brothers and sisters, we agree and believe
In the wondrous union
Of purposed communion[2]

---

[1] Gen. 1:3
[2] stanza 1; Gen. 1:1–2:23

Desired from the great I Am
On the day life first began.
The garden of Eden
Held perfect completion
Until the day they were both deceived.
With sin's awareness, they greatly grieved.
For the serpent remained close at heel,
Always ready to tempt and steal.
Banished from the garden, they sweat,
Tilling the consequence sin beset.[3]
Of Adam and Eve's firstborn sons,
One was good while the other was shunned.
The brothers were named Cain and Abel.
While Abel's walk in God was faithful,
Cain's was stained in dark betrayal
When he buried the one who shared his cradle.
But God's good plan could not be thwarted,
And Adam's seed was still moved forward.
Through the seed of Adam's offspring
Came blessing from a labor's offering.[4]

For in those days, the world turned evil
And did not heed mayhem's upheaval.
God searched and saw in His exam
One who stood an upright man.
Ten descendants from Adam's line,
Noah held to the Lord's align.
So God told Noah to build an ark
For family and creatures to embark.

---

[3] stanza 2; Gen. 3:1–19
[4] stanza 3; Gen. 4:1–5:29

He built and built till it was done;
That was when the floods begun.
And rain it did for forty days
Till the rainbow shone in full display.
A promise earth wouldn't flood again—
A promise forever. Amen and amen![5]

Eleven down from Noah's line,
Abraham was born in God's design.
When it was time, he was found by God.
And to his credit, called friend of God.
When God said, "Go," Abraham went
And gave no argument.
When God said, "Give," he gave,
Even if it meant the grave.
Abraham was willing to sacrifice Isaac,
His son who'd take the name of Israel.
But God never desired to sacrifice humans;
He only required unyielding devotion.[6]

The Lord spared Abraham's son,
For in the end, it was God's own Son—
God's begotten one and only—
To take on sin ransomed solely.
The price He paid to make us holy—
For without, we'd be unholy.
God promised blessing his descendants
To outnumber the stars within his remnant.
For God had chosen the Israelites
With blessing given from heaven's height.[7]

---

[5] stanza 4; Gen. 6:5–9:17, 1 Chron. 1:1–4
[6] stanza 5; Gen. 11:27–12:18
[7] stanza 6; John 3:16, Gen. 22:17, Gen. 12:2, 3

Holy by God and given indeed,
Abraham's line of the chosen seed.
From ancient days of Abraham's line,
Jesus was born of the Lord divine.
God's good, pleasing, and perfect plan
Was in His Son, where the new began.
The new of the covenant would someday replace—
Not to erase, but written in forgiveness and grace.
The chosen seed would be established
In God's great love so freely lavished.[8]

From His sacrifice that testifies
To rise in Him and never die,
It was given to them and given to us
For all who believe in the Lord and trust!
Brothers and sisters, God gives us His Word,
And Genesis is where it first occurs.[9]

---

[8] stanza 7; Gen. 22:16–18, Mt 1:1-17, Heb. 8:8–13
[9] stanza 8; John 3:16–18, Gal. 3:15–29

PROFOUND CALLING
Exodus

"God said to Moses, "I AM WHO I AM" (Exodus 3:14).

"This is my name forever and thus I am to be remembered through all generations" (Exodus 3:16).

As Moses walked, the angel came;
The burning bush became aflame.
In power from the great I Am,
Moses answered, "Here I am".[10]
Then he questioned who exam'ed,
And God said, "I Am who I Am".[11]
I Am your God, who reigns on high.
The Almighty said, It is I.

When Moses proclaimed
The I Am's name,
The "was" was left
And the I Am manifest.
For the Lord provides
And always guides—
Forgiving, kind, and gracious,
Slow to anger through the ages,
Mighty, strong, and righteous,
Yet compassionate in loving kindness.[12]

---

[10] Ex. 3:4
[11] Ex. 3:14
[12] stanza 2; Ex. 2:11–3:15

He is the Lord,
The mighty sword,
The *El Shaddai*
Who sanctifies.
The true and living one
Who was and is and is to come.
He is our banner and our shield,
The faithful one who came to heal.[13]

This God calls out to you and I,
Not in the clouds, but close nearby.
With passion of a burning flame,
He's calling out to you by name.
You were predestined by His call,
For He is God and Lord of all.

Let us stop, take off our shoes,
Listen to His voice and choose
To step onto His holy ground,
Where grace abounds on heaven's crowned.
Praises lift to the renowned:
"I once was lost, but now am found."[14]

---

[13] stanza 3; Ex. 6:2, 3; 31:13; 17:15; 15:26
[14] Hymn, "Amazing Grace," John Newton, 1779

BOOK OF LAW
—————— Leviticus ——————

"Be holy because I, The Lord your God am holy" (Leviticus 19:2).

"You shall be holy to Me, for I The Lord your God am holy and have separated you from the peoples, that you should be mind" (Leviticus 20:26).

"I will make my dwelling among you, and my soul shall not abhor you. And I will walk among you; I will be your God and you will be my people. I am The Lord your God" (Leviticus 20:26).

Leviticus gave divine instruction
When Israel's tribes were summoned.
Spoken by God and penned by Moses,
The Levites vowed in righteous focus:
The law to heed
Was right indeed,
To faithfully observe
And always preserve.
The do's and don'ts were quite precise
In statutes, tithes, and sacrifice.[15]

The statutes were harmonious
In fellowship of holiness.
Extending reconciliation
To bridge the gap of separation,
Guiding Israel and all creation
To the way of true salvation.

---

[15] stanza 1; Lev. 1–7; 19

The symbolic meaning
Was thereby redeeming.[16]

Israel was called to separation
For the sake of preservation.
To set apart the sanctuary
From the common, ordinary,
For God required purification,
Leading to their restoration—
To keep the holy
Holy
And keep the sacred
Sacred.[17]
The Levites worshipped and responded
To keep again the sacred bonded.
They purged the sin that separated
The worldly way from the sacred.
God spoke on how to rightly live
And showed us more of who He is—
How to draw near and how to give—
And gave a promise for all of His.[18]

God showed us we are set apart
In body, mind, and soul and heart.
He called us to Him from the start
To guard our souls and not depart.
So raise your hand in dedication,
And bow before in adoration
To Him who holds His grace in mercy
And in His mercy makes us worthy![19]

---

[16] stanza 2; Lev. 19:37; 4:1–31; 26:3–13
[17] stanza 3; Lev. 19:2; 8:10; 23:27, 28; 10:10; 22:2; Num. 18:32
[18] stanza 4; Lev. 26:44, 45; 26:3–13
[19] stanza 5; Lev. 19:2

BALAAM'S HEART
Numbers

"Behold, I have come out to oppose you because your way is perverse before me. The donkey saw me and turned aside before me these three times. If she had not turned aside from me, surely just now I would have killed you and let her live. Them Balaam said to the angel of The Lord, I have sinned, for I did not know that you stood in the road against me" (Numbers 22:32–35).

What if we answered to the Lord,
"I cannot do anything of my own accord
beyond the command of The Lord"?[20]

What if we answered to the Lord
That by the sixth or seventh time,
We would not turn upon a dime?

What if we answered to the Lord,
"I must only say what God puts in my mouth,"[21]
And never give a mind's eye doubt?

What if we answered to the Lord,
"I can't do anything beyond the command of The Lord,"[22]
And let the truth of God in us restore?

---

[20] Num. 22:18
[21] Num. 22:38
[22] Num. 24:13

What if we answered to the Lord,
His Word in us will not depart
And kept His love within our heart?[23]

What if we answered to the Lord,
And dare to stand in Him alone,
If all other hearts turned to stone?

What if we answered to the Lord,
The greatest treasures ever seen
Mean nothing to the things unseen?[24]

What if we answered to the Lord,
I must do only what God says,[25]
Living the words that Balaam said?

---

[23] Num. 24:15, 16
[24] Num. 23:20, 21; 24:13
[25] Num. 23:26

MT. NEBO
—— Deuteronomy ——

"And you shall remember the whole way that The Lord your God has led you these forty years in the wilderness, that he might humble you, testing you to know what is in your heart, whether you would keep His commandments or not. And He humbled you and let you hunger and fed you with manna, which you did not know, nor did your fathers know, that He might make you know that man does not live by bread alone, but man lives by every word that comes from the mouth of The Lord" (Deuteronomy 8:2–3).

Moses didn't fear
When his end came near.
He wasn't bitter
When he couldn't enter.
He didn't despair
When it seemed unfair.
He wasn't jealous of those who would,
For it was with God that he stood.[26]

He didn't reach the promised land
But viewed it from the borderland.
He saw the dreams that passed him by
When time had come for him to die.
But even Canaan's sweetest land
Could not compare to heaven's plan.
Of all the greatest earthly things,
None beheld the King of kings.[27]

---

[26] stanza 1; Deut. 31:16; 3:23–28; 34:1–9; 39
[27] stanza 2; Deut. 11:11, 12; 32:52; 34:6–12; 8:3

For on that final upward trod,
Peace was found that comes from God.
Moses walked Mt. Nebo's climb;
His eyes were on the Lord's design.
He carried out the final plan
From where his steps first began.
Tried and true, he spoke God's Word,
And all the tribes of Judah heard.[28]

He taught God's laws and statutes
With reverence and with value.
He blessed the younger in his place
And did it with the utmost grace.
Even through the toughest times,
He sought with God to align.
He feared the Lord
And leaned toward.[29]

It was God's will that he pursued
In humility and gratitude.
A faithful, loyal, friend of God
No other dream could ever rob.
His daily interaction
Gave no greater satisfaction
In communion so profound,
Shining down from heaven's crown.[30]

---

[28] stanza 3; Deut. 34:1–4; 6:4–6; 32:1–4; 5:1–22; 4:14
[29] stanza 4; Deut. 4:5–8, 32:24, 25; 3:28; 31:7, 8; 10:12, 13; 20, 21; 13:18
[30] stanza 5; Num. 12:13; Deut. 11:22; 10:10, 11; 30:9, 10

MIRACLES AND MAJESTY
Joshua

"Be strong and courageous. Do not be afraid; do not be discouraged, for The Lord your God will be with you wherever you go" (Joshua 1:9).

Miracles and majesty,
Displayed for all humanity.
Wonders and signs,
By appointment's design.
From wandering through the desert,
To looking upward and overt.
Faithful in the Lord's commands,
In crossing from the borderlands.
The Lord displayed His mighty power,
When the water met His superpower.
Not one remained a doubter,
In the Jordan's parting hour.[31]

Then came the wall of Jericho,
Where once again, God's power showed;
The Lord said, "I will be with you,"
If in God's faith you will pursue,
And march around the city walls,
For giant feats to God are small.
On the seventh day, the walls fell down,
By heaven's wonder who is crowned.
It was God alone who met their call.
And left His promise standing tall.[32]

---

[31] stanza 1; Josh. 3:5; 1:5; 3:9–17; 4:14–24
[32] stanza 2; Josh. 1:5; 1:9; 3:7; 6:1–5; 6:20; 6:27

The Northern kings conspired,
Against the Gibeonites to acquire.
Joshua prayed to direct his army,
And the kings' plans fell sharply;
For God had promised victory,
And Gibeon went down in history.[33]
Joshua prayed for the sun to stand still,
And it was done as it pleased God's will.
The Lord stretched out this wondrous day,
In a miraculous display.
To man it appeared,
The night disappeared,
When dark held off for one more day,
Never had there been such a display.
God confused the kings and riders,
So the enemy couldn't hold its fighters.
Hail rained down from heaven's clouds,
Till all was heard were victory shouts.[34]

Joshua stood by faith and knew,
The Lord above would see him through.
His armor cloaked in loyalty,
With blessing in God's royalty,
Never doubting or afraid,
To trust the Lord and then obey.
He didn't fear who'd stand against,
Knowing God was his defense![35]

---

[33] stanza 3; Josh. 10:3–7; 10:8
[34] stanza 4; Josh. 10:10–14
[35] stanza 5; Josh. 11:15; 23:14; 1:3–9; 23:9–11

FINISHING STRONG
Judges

"Then Sampson prayed to the Lord, 'Sovereign Lord, remember me. Please, God, strengthen me just once more'" (Judges 16:28).

Sampson was a Nazarite,
Ordained by God to stand upright.
Dedicated, consecrated, set apart,
To God who called him in the start.
The Law was strict for Nazarite's.
It was a special vow of right:
No food or drink from on the vine,
A vow to focus at all times.
No contact with an unclean thing,
Set apart for the King of Kings.
No razor blade to touch the head,
An outward sign of lives they led.[36]

Samson's strength was beyond compare,
So long a blade didn't touch his hair.
He conquered beasts with his bare hands,
While walking in the borderlands.
He killed a thousand in the Philistine's command,
With a donkey's jawbone in his hand.
Then sat a judge for twenty years,
Though lacking in his daily prayers.
His dedication lacked devotion,
And worship slid on the erosion.
For he knew it broke a promise,

---

[36] stanza 1; Judg. 13:3–5; 13:12–14; 13:4; 13:24, 25; Num. 6:2, 3; 6:7, 8

When he touched the unclean carcass.
His authority lacked accountability,
With the given weight of responsibility.
He fraternized with the enemy,
Though it stepped on the decree.
He casually walked through the vineyard,
A sign his walk with God was hindered.
Inflated with esteem of self,
The way in which the flesh compels.
For only after time and length,
He told the vow that held his strength.
He mistook God's great patience,
For His affirmation in the silence.
And then one day it finally happened,
Though unaware and gravely challenged;[37]

The day the Lord's Spirit left him.
Oh sad the day when hope grew dim.
The enemy joined to rob his sight,
But eternal sight was given in spite.
In heart's repentance and soul's dependence,
He sought the Lord and prayed for vengeance.
Samson raised to God and prayed, "Remember me again,"
Oh, sovereign God, let me have this one last win.
His hands crushed the pillars with the Philistines,
When the temple collapsed to smithereens.
In the final act of Samson's life,
His soul again became alive.[38]

---

[37] stanza 2; Judg. 16:17; 14:5, 6; 15:15, 16; 15:20; 14:5; 15:3, 4; 14:8, 9; 14:10; 15:17; 16:4–17; Num. 6:6; 6:2–4

[38] stanza 3; Judg. 16:20, 21; 16:28–30

THE HEART OF A SERVANT
Ruth

"May The Lord, the God of Israel, under whose wings you have come to take refuge, reward you fully for what you have done" (Ruth 2:12).

Ruth served the Lord
With a servant's heart.
And in serving the Lord,
She did not depart.

In faith, she trusted,
Sharing a burden.
In love, she entrusted,
Selfless in Him.
In oath to Naomi,
Gracious and kind,
To ever be.
Ruth's words to bind:

"Where you go,
I will go.
And where you stay,
I will stay.
Your people
Will be my people
And your God,
My God.
Where you die,
I will die
And there, I will be buried."[39]

---

[39] Ruth 1:16, 17

That oath, she carried,
Committing in full,
Never once looking back.
Her hands never dull,
While she gleaned the stacks,
In the harvesting field.[40]
She worked for Boaz, to whom it belonged.
He was in the line of her family shield,[41]
And before too long,
She uncovered his feet,
As custom was then.[42]
All part of God's plan, while gathering wheat!
A shoe then traded instead of a pen[43]
And Boaz took Ruth to be his wife.[44]
God gave them a son,
Renewing their life—
For born of their son,
King David was born![45]

---

[40] Ruth 2:2–7
[41] Ruth 2:19, 20
[42] Ruth 3:1–9
[43] Ruth 4:7–11
[44] Ruth 4:13
[45] Ruth 4:18–22

THE COVENANT OF THE LORD
I Samuel

"Don't be afraid, Samuel reassured them. You have certainly done wrong, but make sure now that you worship The Lord with all your heart, and don't turn your back on Him. Don't go back to worshiping worthless idols that cannot help or rescue you, they are totally useless! The Lord will not abandon his people, because that would dishonor his great name. For it has pleased The Lord to make you his very own people" (Samuel 12:20–22).

The Lord our God is ever holy.
His covenant stands ever boldly.
In times of old, housed in the ark,
The word of God, to all embarked.
Taught by the Lord, His chosen ones,
They were His own and called them sons.
But sons and daughters turned their backs
And robbers came up in attack.
For godless idols they replaced,
And the ark was stolen from its place.
They let the word of God depart,
Believing lies that robbed their heart.
In time the holy ark returned,
And Israel's heart again was turned.
Singing songs renewed in voice,
Praise to God they did rejoice![46]

---

[46] stanza 1; 1 Sam. 4:4, 5; 2:12; 4:11–22; 6:10–13; 7:3, 4

The ark now housed within the heart,
Always to be set apart!
His written Word dwells within,
By the Lord, who's always been!
But time again we're under attack,
We lose our focus and fall off track.
We build an ark, not of the Lord,
And in rebellion, drop His sword.
But Samuel sternly told King Saul;
Obey the Lord lest sin befall,[47]

Glory to God who carries in grace,
To be with Him in His holy place.
His mercy guides us to the light.
And jealous love for us will fight,
He'll claim us in His sovereign Word,
And refine us of all that's blurred.
So serve Him with a brand-new start,
Let none besides lay hold your heart.
Let now our heart His name proclaim,
And come and live in His domain.
Follow closely His decrees,
And stand for Him who sets us free![48]

---

[47] stanza 2; 1 Sam. 15:22, 23; 12:14–25
[48] stanza 3; 1 Sam. 16:5; 30:23

TRUSTING GOD
2 Samuel

"Trust in the hand of The Lord and not in the hand of flesh" (2 Samuel 8:4).

Stories unfolded through the pages,
Of trusting God, the Lord Most High.
Godly men throughout the ages,
Not so unlike you and I.
In times of past and of today,
We look for strength within our hands,
Stumbling from His truth and way.
But God alone eternally stands,
And arms us by the Spirit's sword.[49]

David sought the Lord's own heart.
He knew by trusting God he'd win,
But still, he let God's Word depart,
By taking a census and thus did sin.
He took a count of men to fight,
Failing to trust the strength of God's hand.
He lost a moment of spiritual sight,
When seeking strength on his own to stand.[50]

Uzzah, like David, knew the Lord.
He knew God's law not to touch the ark.
But relied on himself to hold and restore,
The ox that stumbled from the embarked.
He used his hand to steady the ark,

---

[49] stanza 1; 2 Sam. 22:31; 22:47
[50] stanza 2; 2 Sam. 22:29; 24:1–4; 24:10

Failing to trust God's hand was enough.
And in that moment, God's judgment sparked,
For then and now, God's hand is enough![51]

Oh, Lord, You are the one we call.
Your strength and power's always been!
You are the one who's conquered all.
Help us find your strength again.[52]

"Your covenant is trustworthy." [53]
I will trust in you and not be afraid.
Open our eyes in You to see,
You are the Rock on which I'm stayed![54]

---

[51] stanza 3; Num. 4:15; 19:20; Ex. 25:13–16; 1 Chron. 13:9, 10; 2 Sam. 6:6, 7
[52] stanza 4; 2 Sam. 22:2–4; 22:47; 6:14
[53] 2 Sam. 7:28
[54] stanza 5; 2 Sam. 22:31, 32; 7:22–29

SOFT WHISPERS
1 Kings

"After the earthquake, came a fire, but The Lord was not in the fire. And after the fire came a gentle whisper. When Elijah heard it, he pulled his cloak over his face then a voice said to him, What are you doing here Elijah?" (1 Kings 19:12–13).

The hurricane came,
But You were not in it.
The earthquake trembled,
But You were not in it.
The fire blazed through,
But again, You were not in it.[55]

Instead You came in a gentle whisper,
Calling us back to You again.
Gently, You whispered, where are you?
And called us back to You again.
Your soft and gentle prompting,
Turns our hearts to You again.
Even when we've run from You,
Your love returns us, once again.[56]

Storms may come, and winds may rise.
But even so, the heart that's wise—
Is the heart that listens to Your call,
Amidst the trials that befall
And drowns out all the other noise,
To heed the prompting of Your voice.[57]

---

[55] stanza 1; 1 Kings 19:11, 12
[56] stanza 2; 1 Kings 19:12, 13
[57] stanza 3; 1 Kings 19:14–16

FAITH TO SEE
2 Kings

"And Elisha prayed, 'Oh Lord, open his eyes so he may see'. Then The Lord opened the servant's eyes and he looked and saw the hills full of horses and chariots of fire all around Elisha'" (2 Kings 6:17).

Elisha was not gripped with fear,
When the enemy drew near.
Surrounding danger threatened wide,
Closing in from every side.[58]

Panic filled the servant's heart,
But peace remained in the prophet's heart.
Elisha stood in confidence,
Seeing God's omnipotence.

He prayed his servant's eyes to see
The strong and mighty hand of Thee.
God touched his eyes and he saw higher!
Horses and chariots and flames of fire;[59]

The enemy was completely confused,
And there again, God's power proved!
No sword was drawn, no blood did pour,
The day that Aram waged a war![60]

---

[58] stanza 1; 2 Kings 6:15, 16
[59] stanza 3; 2 Kings 6:17
[60] stanza 4; 2 Kings 6:18–23

Oh, Lord, we pray our faith to rise,
When fear surrounds, "open our eyes."
The times in which attack surrounds,
We pray Your Word is firmly bound!

Let Your voice be what we hear
And peace rise up above the fear!
For Satan's ploys will not prevail,
Our God, our shield, will never fail![61]

---

[61] stanza 6; Rom. 8:31–33

WHEN GOD ANSWERS NO
I Chronicles

"Listen to me my brothers and my people. I had it in my heart to build a house as a place of rest for the ark of the covenant of The Lord, for the footstool of our God, and I made plans to build it, but God said to me, You are not to build a house for my Name, because you are a warrior and have shed blood" (1 Chronicles 28:2–3).

"David also said to Solomon his son, Be strong and courageous, and do the work. Do not be afraid or discouraged, for The Lord God, my God, is with you. He will not fail you or forsake you until all the work for the service of the temple of The Lord is finished" (1 Chronicles 28:20).

In David's heart was great desire.
A dream in time, he had acquired.
To build the Lord a sacred temple.
Where God's presence came to settle.
And though all heaven can't contain,
He dreamed a house where God would reign.
His motives were pure, to honor the Lord,
But David a warrior, shed blood by the sword.
God answered no, for his hands weren't the ones.
Instead it would be the hands of his son.[62]

---

[62] stanza 1; 1 Chron. 17:1; 22:6, 7; 28:2; 18:1–14; 28:3; 17:4; 22:7, 8; 2 Chron. 6:18; 2:5, 6; 2 Sam. 7:1–13

So David passed his dream to Solomon,
To build the house when his day was done.
David's hope did not despair. Instead
He knew that God is the head.
The Lord is God of heaven and earth,
The one who spoke creation's birth.
He is the King of all good things,
To that, David bowed and exalted him King![63]

---

[63] stanza 2; 1 Chron. 22:5–9; 28:1–10; 17:16–24; 29:3–5; 29:10–20; Gen. 1:1

NO OTHER IDOLS
2 Chronicles

"The Lord is with you when you are with him. If you seek him, he will be found by you, but if you forsake him, he will forsake you" (2 Chronicles 15:2).

The royalty of David's line—
Israel's chosen, blessed bind.
Descendants of the kings to reign.
From Solomon to Cyrus that became,
The kings of biblical times.
Some followed God's perfect design.
They looked to God for Him to lead,
And chose His sovereign Word to heed![64]

But some forgot God's promises,
And other idols, chose to kiss.
Pages in the scriptures see,
The gripping power of pride to be.
For sin too often does repeat,
Down the path to pride's defeat.[65]

---

[64] stanza 1; Matt. 1:1–6; 2 Chron. 36:22, 23; Isa. 44:28; Isa. 45:1–6; 2 Chron. 1:7–12; 31:20, 21

[65] stanza 2; 2 Chron. 36:11–16; 26:16–18; Shmoop editorial team, "The good kings of Judah in 2 Chronicles," November 11, 2008

So do not let His Word depart,
Remove the idols of the heart—
All that causes you to stumble,
Rid your heart, be ever humble!
Seek Him always in one accord,
He is the everlasting Lord!
The Lord is with you,
His words are true;
"When you seek Me,
You will find Me."[66][67]

---

[66] 2 Chron. 15:2
[67] stanza 3; 2 Chron. 7:19, 20; 7:14, 15; 31:21; 20:15

TRUE REPENTANCE
Ezra

"When the builders completed the foundation of The Lord's temple, the priest put on their robes and took their places to blow their trumpets. And the Levites clashed their cymbals to praise The Lord, just as king David had. With praise and thanks, they sang this song to The Lord: He is so good" (Ezra 3:10).

After seventy years
Israel returned
From captivity's fears.
Together they yearned,
To rebuild the temple—
Ruined in past, from long ago.
Judah gathered into assemble,
And work began even though
Three years and some, it'd take.
The foundation now laid,
The people rejoiced, with souls awake.
They sang with shouts to God and prayed.
Trumpets blew throughout the land!
Though foreigners opposed attempts to rebuild,
Judah held firm and took a stand,
For God anointed the hands of the skilled![68]

Ezra arrived, well versed in the law,
A descendant himself of Moses's line.
He taught the scriptures with reverence and awe.
Instilling in them, God's wonders and signs.

---

[68] stanza 1; Jer. 29:10–14; Ezr 1:5, Ezr 3:8-13, Ezr 4:3-5

But past the temple walls, he saw
It wasn't the building that needed repair,
But the heart that was in need of God's law.
He cried out to Judah full of despair,
For over time, the people had strayed!
Ezra tore his robe in mourning and prayer
And in repentance, they fasted and prayed,
For living without God was too much to bear![69]

(Ezra's Prayer)
Our iniquities' are piled high!
How can we ever face You?
Our guilt reaches to the sky,
So thick, we can't see You!
Please do not forsake us now
You've seen our guilt with Your own eye.
Today in You, we renew our vow!
Your word is truth, none can deny![70]

All of Judah responded together,
Renewing their love in one accord.
Faithful to God, and not fair-weathered.
Proclaiming to God, that He is The Lord![71]

---

[69] stanza 2; Ezra 7:5–10; 7:25; 9:1–5; 10:6; Neh. 2:11
[70] stanza 3; Ezra 9:6–15
[71] stanza 4; Neh. 8:9, 12

LEADING THE PEOPLE
Nehemiah

"O Lord, let your ear be attentive to the prayer of this your servant [Nehemiah] and to the prayer of your servants who delight in revering your name" (Nehemiah 1:11).

Delighted he was, in revering God's name,
Oh, that we'd, too, delight in His name![72]

Living out loud in holy example,
His hands and heart, to God ever ample.
Nehemiah prayed to God for direction,
Oh, that we'd, too, pray for direction![73]

He worked by trade with stone and mortar,
Rebuilding the wall of Israel's border!
Nehemiah entrusted his heart to the Lord,
Oh, that we'd, too, trust in the Lord![74]
The breath he was given had higher purpose,
For the labor of sweat was only the surface!
Nehemiah remembered God's covenant of love,
Oh, that we'd, too, remember His love![75]

---

[72] stanza 1; Neh. 1:11
[73] stanza 2; Neh. 6:9; 4:21
[74] stanza 3; Neh. 5:16
[75] stanza 4; Neh. 13:1–31; 9:7, 8

He strengthened the hearts and minds that he led,
Knowing the work was holy and sacred.
Nehemiah prayed for strength in his work,
Oh, that we'd, too, pray for strength in our work![76]

Enemies pressed to destroy them as one,
And builders grew weary of work to be done!
Nehemiah set watchmen to stay on guard.
Oh, that we'd, too, be ready on guard![77]

Deceivers tried to lead him astray,
But he knew their way wasn't the Way!
Nehemiah's steps were in the Lord.
Oh, that we'd, too, take our steps in the Lord![78]

He fasted and prayed, seeking God's will,
And in God's presence, his spirit was filled!
Nehemiah prayed by night and by day,
Oh, that we'd, too, pray by night and by day![79]

Discouraged, they said, we can't build this wall,
But knowing, he led and answered the call!
Nehemiah corrected the sin in their way.
Oh, that we'd, too, be correct in the Way![80]
He called to account, the ones who had wondered.
Instilling God's presence is here to be honored.
Nehemiah praised God in glory Most High,
Oh, that we'd, too, praise our God Most High![81]

---

[76] stanza 5; Neh. 6:9
[77] stanza 6; Neh. 4:10–14
[78] stanza 7; Neh. 6:8–13; 9:32
[79] stanza 8; Neh. 1:4–6
[80] stanza 9; Neh. 4:10; 5:8, 9
[81] stanza10; Neh. 13:11–30; 9:5

For "the Joy of the Lord is our strength"[82]
In wisdom he saw eternity's length!
Nehemiah's thoughts were heaven-bound.
Oh, that our thoughts would be heaven-bound!

A living prayer from within he prayed,
Encouraging men as the bricks were laid.
Nehemiah lived each day in the Spirit.
Oh, that we'd, too, live in the Spirit![83]

He taught with Ezra, God's holy Word,
From dawn until dusk till everyone heard!
Nehemiah shared in God's holy Word.
Oh, that we'd, too, share in His Word![84]

He led his life and people in prayer;
Pray, then work, and the wall was repaired!
Nehemiah's faith unwavered in strength.
Oh, that we'd, too, have faith of that strength![85]

Their joy in the Lord led them to praise,
They sung out to God in victory raised.
Across the land, their joy was made known,
Oh, that our joy would also be known![86]

---

[82] Neh. 8:10
[83] stanza 12; Neh. 4:14; 9:5
[84] stanza 13; Neh. 8:9
[85] stanza 14; Neh. 6:9; 8:10
[86] stanza 15; Neh. 12:43

COURAGE IN FAITH
Esther

"And who knows but that you have come to a royal position for such a time as this" (Esther 4:14).

Esther was orphaned as a young child.
Her life though crafted in beauty beguiled.
Esther through Mordecai had family ties,
And Mordecai stepped up with a father's eye.
He raised her as if she was his daughter.
Molded and shaped through the hands of the potter!
They lived in Persia where Xerxes was king,
And he was searching for a new queen.[87]

Esther, now grown, was shown to the king,
And he promptly gave her a wedding ring.
She lived within the royal courts,
But loyal to Mordecai, she kept rapport.
Mordecai's faith stood solid and deep,
He led God's people in their faith to keep.
In reverence, he bowed only to God,
Instilling with reverence, God's power and awe.[88]

Evil took root in the high ranking Haman,
When he was promoted second-in-command.
He harbored plans to ruin God's own,
Deceiving the king with a heart of stone.

---

[87] stanza 1; Est. 2:6, 7; 1:1; 2:2–4
[88] stanza 2; Est. 2:8; 2:16–18; 2:5, 6; 4:5, 6; 3:4

He ordered the people to bow down and kneel,
In an attempt by power and pride to steal.[89]

Mordecai stood outside the court's gates,
Standing for God instead of law's 'fate'.
He refused in faith to bow to another,
For his conviction of faith couldn't be covered.
Haman vowed to kill every Jew.
Seeking glory in his own eyes view.[90]

Mordecai sought rescue from heaven above.
He cried out to God, affirming His love,
Petitioning his case through fasting and prayer,
For God in His mercy, their lives to be spared.
Esther pled mercy seeking the Way.
She gathered women in the court to pray,[91]

Keeping the Lord to her ever near.
She refused in faith to turn a deaf ear.
She knew in her heart, God's King over all,
And carefully planned to heed His call.
With courage in faith, she prayed for a way
And was extended the specter the following day.[92]

---

[89] stanza 3; Est. 3:1–11
[90] stanza 4; Est. 2:5; 4:2, 3; 3:2; 3:8, 9
[91] stanza 5; Est. 4:12–14; 4:1–3; 4:15
[92] stanza 6; Est. 5:3

She invited to dinner both friend and foe,
But it wasn't time for God's plan to show.
Wisely, she waited with God's Word in her,
Refusing to let the timing deter.
She invited again, to expose the wrong,
And it all came to light before too long.[93]

Haman's plot of evil then surfaced,
And the king reversed all he had purposed.
Many that day put their trust in the Lord.
Upon them divinely God's blessing was poured![94]

---

[93] stanza 7; Est. 5:4–8; 7:3–6
[94] stanza 8; Est. 7:4; 8:2; 8:16, 17

HEAVEN WISE
— Job —

"I know that my Redeemer lives, and that in the end, He will stand on the earth. And after my skin has been destroyed, yet in my flesh I will see God; I myself will see Him with my own eyes—I, and not another. How my heart yearns within me" _(Job 19:25–27).

A blameless pure and upright man,
None was like him in the land.
Satan challenged the faith of Job—
In evil schemes of epic probe.
Integrity pushed into the dark,
In surmounting trials to embark.[95]

Job's sons and daughters were all taken,
Still, his faith remained unshaken.
His skin and bones were torment-bound,
Relief was nowhere to be found.
The deceiver came and stripped away.
In holiness, Job kneeled and prayed;[96]
"Naked I came from my mother's womb,
And naked I shall return.
The Lord gave and the Lord took away,
Blessed be the name of The Lord."[97]

---

[95] stanza 1; Job 1:1; 1:9–19; 2:4–7
[96] stanza 2; Job 1:18, 19; 2:7, 8
[97] stanza 3; Job 1:21

Oh, may we have the faith of Job
And not lose sight of heaven's hope.
His faith was in the Lord's assurance
And trusted God's deliverance.
Job voiced the praise he had to give:
"I know that my Redeemer lives!"[98][99]

His hope was in the Lord's perfection,
In the final change of resurrection.
Job's spoken thoughts were heaven wise,
He knew he'd see God with his eyes.
His confidence held certainty.
True justice lies eternally.[100]
The Lord our God is our Redeemer,
The strong and mighty vindicator!
Job took his stance to defend,
And God above called him friend.[101]

---

[98] Job 19:25
[99] stanza 4; Job 13:16
[100] stanza 5; Job 14:14; 19:6
[101] stanza 6; Job 42:12; 17:19; 4:17; 23:10–12; 2:2

PURSUING GOD
Psalms

"I love the house where You live, O Lord, the place where your glory dwells" (Psalm 26:8).

"One thing I ask of The Lord, this is what I seek: That I may dwell in the house of The Lord forever" (Psalm 27:4).

"I have seen you in the sanctuary and beheld your power and your glory. Because your love is better than life, my lips will glorify you. I will praise you as long as I live, and in your name I will lift up my hands. My soul will be satisfied" (Psalm 63:2–5).

"Your love is better than life" (Psalm 63:3).

A shepherd boy
Of servant heart.
God's hand employed
A work of art.
With staff and sling,
In early days;
He graced the strings
And sought God's way.[102]

He knew the Lord
Would see him through,
Whatever lay in store.
And though his rivals grew,
Still, he offered up his praise.

---

[102] stanza 1; Ps. 16:11–21

He looked for help from God above,
And then his humble heart was raised
To God's unfailing love.[103]

With sling and stone,
Goliath fell,
And God was made known,
When the Philistine's fell!
Saul, though king,
Had ill repute
And envy took a swing.
He charged full speed in hot pursuit,
And anger showed no mercy.
But David forgave Saul instead,
And God's anointing flipped inversely,
The day the crown was placed on David's head![104]

David pursued
The heart of God!
Hope and faith held true,
In spite of human flaws!
He found a place in mercy's seat,
Assured salvation's by the one
Who sees His work's complete.
David knew truth already'd won,[105]

For it's God who throws sin in the sea,
And God alone who pardons sin!
By faith, he knew someday he'd see,
Heaven's perfection, opened within!
For though he wore an earthly crown,
He knew the worth of heaven's gain.

---

[103] stanza 2; Ps. 9:10; 17:6, 7; 86:12, 13
[104] stanza 3; Ps. 17:41–50; 18:10, 11; 1 Sam. 15:29; 2 Sam. 12:30
[105] stanza 4; 1 Sam. 13:14; Acts 13:22; Ps. 115:1; 57:2; 118:14–24

Salvation's glory will astound,
By God enthroned who holy reigns![106]

When came the time of latter days,
David lifted fervent prayer—
Praise bestowed to Him who saves,
Honor to God his voice declared![107]

---

[106] stanza 5; Ps. 103:12; 5:7; 63:3; Mic. 7:19; Isa. 43:25; Heb. 10:17, 18
[107] stanza 6; Ps. 103:1–22

THE PATH
Proverbs

"The fear of The Lord is the foundation of true knowledge" (Proverbs 1:7).

The straight path,
Is narrow, alas.
The wise direction,
Brings higher connection.
Wisdom's the key,
God's guarantee.
Prayer guides our feet,
To be complete.[108]

The holy road
Will not erode.
Follow the Lord,
With His Word stored.
His peace instills,
Through valleys and hills.
For wisdom's knowledge,
Keeps footing solid.[109]

Walk not in foolish company,
But keep wise friends abundantly.
Watch warnings and be heedful
To keep your feet from evil.

---

[108] stanza 1; Prov. 8:35; 1:5, 6; 2:2–9
[109] stanza 2; Prov. 30:5; 14:12; 15:24; 9:10; 4:5–9

Hold truth secure,
Till footing's sure.
True wisdom heeds correction,
With mindful redirection,
It offers a hand,
When friends disband.[110]

Walk in the light.
Do not lose fight
In heart, hold fast
Till home at last.[111]

---

[110] stanza 3; Prov. 22:24, 25; 23:19; 27:17; 1:15, 16; 4:26, 27; 3:5, 6; 10:9; 28:18; 3:11, 12; 28:23; 9:9; 24:17, 18

[111] stanza 4; Prov. 16:1; 13:25; 20:27; 21:21

PURPOSED DAYS
Ecclesiastes

"Fear God and keep all His commands, for this is the duty of all mankind. For God will bring every deed into judgment, including every hidden thing, whether it is good or evil" (Ecclesiastes 12:13–14).

How dark a place
When thoughts disgrace
And turn upon itself.
The mind does dwell
And so does find,
A dark and empty blind.
All of time
Isn't worth a dime,
If only lived for self![112]
The highest stock of earthly wealth,
Is only stored in vain.
It has no worth in heaven's gain,
No matter toil or strain.[113]
Desire wisdom, to obtain,
Eyes to see what will remain.[114]
For when the eyes of focus shift,
God's presence clearly does exist![115]
The aimless burden He by lifts,
When to the Lord our hearts commit!

---

[112] Eccl. 1:1–8
[113] Eccl. 2:10, 11
[114] Eccl. 7:19
[115] Eccl. 8:1

There beholds the meaning of life
And in it we become alive![116]
In work and toil, fun and play,
Remember to give thanks and pray.[117]
To God alone, give highest praise,
For God has purposed every day!

---

[116] Eccl. 5:18–20
[117] Eccl. 12:13, 14

BLESSED UNION
Song of Songs

"Many waters cannot quench love, nor can rivers drown it. If a man tried to buy love with all of his wealth, his offer would be utterly scorned" (Song of Solomon 8:7).

Oh, blessed the union
Of fellowship's communion.
His love by which, none can compare,
The Lord, our God, Himself declares.[118]

Not water, fire, even death,
Can quench the flame within the depth.
A love so strong, it can't relent,
And shares the touch of His imprint.[119]

He breathed His love within our being,
And long before, His love preceding.
By wonder of love's holy blessing,
The heart will cling and hold its dwelling.[120]

And so the two repeat, "I do,"
With greater love to ensue.
Hearts are joined in one accord
By beauty woven in the Lord.[121]

---

[118] stanza 1; Song 1:1; 2:16; Isa. 54:5; Rev. 19:6–8
[119] stanza 2; Song 8:6, 7
[120] stanza 3; Song 3:5
[121] stanza 4; Song 3:11

Sacred bond, together one,
Through the Father's holy Son.
There delights beyond all measure,
Together with the one you treasure.[122]

Hearts beheld in one accord,
A woven cord within the Lord.
His love in us will purify,
And to His name be glorified![123]

Freedom's found within His love,
In holy presence from above.
The heart and spirit of mankind,
In Christ forever more aligned![124]

---

[122] stanza 5; Isa. 61:10; Song 2:10
[123] stanza 6; Song 6:3; 7:10
[124] stanza 7; Rev. 22:17

HOLY, HOLY, HOLY!
Isaiah

"I saw The Lord, high and exalted, seated on a throne; and the train of His robe filled the temple. Above Him were seraphim, each with six wings: With two wings they covered their faces, with two they covered their feet and with two they were flying. And they were calling to one another: Holy, holy, holy is The Lord Almighty; the whole earth is full of His glory" (Isaiah 6:1–3).

Isaiah anointed,
By God appointed.
His name's translation:
"The Lord is salvation!"
Isaiah foretold,
In visions bestowed—
God's greatness displayed,
In splendor arrayed.
His holiness shone,
On His governing throne.
Angels surrounded,
The echoes resounded—
Praises to the one and only:
"Holy, holy, holy
Is the Lord God Almighty,"[125]
Crowned above divinely![126]

---

[125] Isa. 6:3
[126] stanza 1; Isa. 6:1–7

The sight of God
Captured his thoughts
As the train of His robe
Caused inward probe.
Isaiah humbled himself thereby,
And said to the Lord, "Here am I."[127]
Salvation revealed its sacrifice,
Then God above he glorified.
Faithfully, he brought the light,
With hope and faith to ignite,
For Israel had gone astray
And faith was far away.
He called to turn their hearts around,
And lead the lost to then be found,
Where deaf and blindness bred,
And defiance was widespread.
Rebellion was with fury,
But God would not lay down His glory!
Zealously, the Lord pursued,
And by His power so refused,
To let His holy sanctuary
Be treated ordinary![128]

The Lord is His name,
And His truth remains.
In His salvation,
He called to awaken,
Cleansing His chosen
In holy devotion!
God's love surpassed
All His wrath.

---

[127] Isa. 6:8

[128] stanza 2; Isa. 6:5; 6:1; 12:2; 63:7; 8:13–17; 1:4; 43:10–13; 6:9; 1:2; 17:7–10; 42:8

He rebuilt the upheaval,
To strengthen His people.
He is the Redeemer
Of every believer!
He's the First and the Last,
His love unsurpassed.
For beyond all measure,
Our heart is His treasure![129]

---

[129] stanza 3; Isa. 5:16; 61:10, 11; 46:3, 4; 49:8; 49:16; 29:16; 40:29–31; 30:18; 56:1, 2; 44:6; 49:11; 55:1, 2; 35:8–10

YAHWEH WILL LIFT UP
———————— Jeremiah ————————

"But if you say 'I will not mention His word or speak anymore in His name', His word is in my heart like a fire, a fire shut up in my bones. I am weary of holding it in; indeed, I cannot" (Jeremiah 20:9).

"The days are coming, declares The Lord, when I will make a new covenant with the people of Israel and with the people of Judah. It will not be like the covenant I made with their ancestors when I took them by the hand to lead them out of Egypt, because they broke my covenant, though I was a husband to them. This is the covenant I will make with the people of Israel after that time, declares The Lord, I will put my new law in their minds and write it in their hearts. I will be their God, and they will be my people" (Jeremiah 31:31).

Judah's later prophet
lived his life voicing caution
In a decaying nation
That needed restoration.[130]

Born of a priestly line,
Prestige he left behind.
His call was at a price,
Denying self in sacrifice.[131]

---

[130] stanza 1; Jer. 3:6–9
[131] stanza 2; Jer. 1:1

Through the Lord, he testified,
Though his family left his side.
Friends alike, turned their back,
Set against him in attack.[132]
He stood alone.
No family his own,
To share his load,
On the days bestowed.[133]

Discouraged and lonely,
But still, preaching boldly.
He sought discernment,
Amidst discouragement.[134]

Forsaken by all,
Yet true to his call.
His words were refused,
But still he pursued.[135]
Seeming to fail,
From Israel's denial.
Rejected by man,
But not in God's plan![136]

A witness as called,
Even though mauled.
When evil sought to prosper,
God revealed He is the potter.[137]

---

[132] stanza 3; Jer. 15:10
[133] stanza 4; Jer. 15:17; 16:2
[134] stanza 5; Jer. 7:2–7; 10:23, 24
[135] stanza 6; Jer. 12:6; 1:5; 16:1–21
[136] stanza 7; Jer. 15:15–21; 1:10
[137] stanza 8; Jer. 37:14, 15; 18:1–6

The true and righteous Cornerstone,
Is Christ alone who sits enthroned;
He breathed His Spirit,
Upon His witness.[138]

Where grace revealed,
As the prophet kneeled.
In truth's decree,
He could foresee,
And said unto Thee,
I heard and now see.[139]

In visions heightened,
He couldn't keep silent.
Fire burning deep within,
God's Spirit moved in him.[140]

He saw beyond captivity,
And suffering's longevity.
Past the dungeon's shackles,
To grace beyond expansions![141]

In the beautiful prediction,
Of the coming resurrection!
New hope and glory
In love's great story![142]

---

[138] stanza 9; Isa. 28:16; Jer. 1:9,10
[139] stanza 10; Jer. 15:16
[140] stanza 11; Jer. 1:11–14; 18:1–6; 24; 20:9
[141] stanza 12; Jer. 23:5, 6
[142] stanza 13; Jer. 33:3

A new covenant given,
In God's provision.
Instead of tablets or a scroll,
Written in our heart and soul.[143]

Instead of foreign rituals,
A one-on-one relationship.
Instead of condemnation,
The gift of reconciliation.[144]

The promise of the potter told,
Extolling beauty to behold.
A marvel only He could fathom
by the hands of His compassion.[145]

Holding us in His grace,
As we turn to seek His face.
He'll bring us back to Him again
And restore us once again. Amen![146]

---

[143] stanza 14; Jer. 31:31–34; 32:28–41; 50:5
[144] stanza 15; Jer. 31:1–9
[145] stanza 16; Jer. 18:1–6
[146] stanza 17; Jer. 17:7

THE LORD RESTORES
(Double Acrostic)
— Lamentations —

"Because of The Lord's great love we are not consumed, for His compassion never fails. They are new every morning; great is your faithfulness. I say to myself, The Lord is my portion; therefore I will wait for Him" (Lamentations 3:22–24).

Lament, for we are sinful.[147]
Abandon all the sin and go.[148]
Mourn the sin and turn it over.[149]
Earnestly seek His grace to rebuild.
Never forget the Lord your maker.[150]
The holy Lord will come to avenge,[151]
And He will restore what is His.[152]
Turn and seek to know His heart,[153]
In lieu of things that come and go.[154]
One day we'll stand at heaven's door.[155]
New hope in glory to Him raise—
Salvation from the Lord invites![156]

---

[147] Lam. 2:18
[148] Lam. 2:19
[149] Lam. 1:20
[150] Lam. 5:19
[151] Lam. 2:22
[152] Lam. 5:21
[153] Lam. 3:40
[154] Lam. 4:1
[155] Lam. 3:31, 32
[156] Lam. 3:22–25

REBORN
Ezekiel

"I will give them an undivided heart and put a new spirit in them; I will remove from their heart of stone and give them a heart of flesh. Then they will be careful to keep my laws. They will be my people, and I will be the God" (Ezekiel 11:19–20).

Fearlessly faithful,
All while in exile.
By mission a witness,
To bridge reconcile.[157]

A watchman for his people,
Called by God to bring attention
Where roots ran deep in sin's rebellion
And brought the nation to upheaval.[158]

The Lord revealed His sovereignty,
From heaven's realm in highest court—
In power's judging supremacy,
To rid the pathway of distort.[159]

Vision's bestowed a window's eye,
To what an eye cannot behold.
The splendor of His glory lies,
In heaven's glimpse of praise extol.[160]

---

[157] stanza 1; Ezek. 1:1
[158] stanza 2; Ezek. 3:17–21; 2:3
[159] stanza 3; Ezek. 28:25; 43:8, 9
[160] stanza 4; Ezek. 1:26–28; 3:23; 43:2–5

Past the awe of whirls and wheels,
God's message plain and simple:
Through all time the Lord reveals,
And will bring us to His holy temple.[161]

Out from where the bones lay piled
From the grave of godless state.
For only God and God alone,
Can breathe in life and recreate.[162]

---

[161] stanza 5; Ezek. 1:15–24
[162] stanza 6; Ezek. 37:1–14

COURAGE DEFINED
Daniel

"If we are thrown into the blazing furnace, the God we serve is able to deliver us from it, and He will deliver us from your majesty's hand. But even if He does not, we want you to know, Your Majesty, that we will not serve your gods or worship the image of gold you have set up" (Daniel 3:17–18).

A Bible story told again,
Daniel in the lion's den.
In a prideful state of self,
The king demanded more than wealth
And ordered prayers be prayed to him,
Or be thrown in the lion's den!
The law was clear and gave no choice.
Though troubled, still, he held his poise,
And at his word, the kings own men,
Threw Daniel in the lion's den!
Then God displayed His mighty hand;
Under which, no man could stand.
He shut the jaws of lion's mouths
And kept him from the lion's pounce!
Daniel stood with them unarmed,
And not a hair on him was harmed!
God sent his angels to protect
By perfect plan to intersect;
For then the king acknowledged God,
And said, The Lord's the living God![163]

---

[163] stanza 1; Dan. 6:1–28

And then there were the faithful three,
Fated by the kings' decree.
King Nebuchadenzzer'
Statue ensnared;
Ninety feet high and nine feet wide,
Built with solid gold and pride!
Shadrack, Meshack, and Abednego
Refused to bow their heads down low.
To do would be ungodly praise,
With consequence of fire's blaze,
Of all who would not worship him,
Even though it'd be a sin!
In faith they bowed to God's great name,
And said God saves and God alone!
Even when the stakes were high,
They refused to run and hide!
Shadrack, Meshack, and Abednego
Couldn't see what would bestow.
Still they said, God is able, but even so—
We will never serve your gods below![164]
They knew the Lord would prevail,
Despite the king's own travail.
In hostile, angry, rampant claims,
He sentenced death by fire's flames.
The three were bound and thrown in,
By the king's own prideful sin.
The furnace burned bright and hot!
But, despite the evil king's laid plot,
And also to the guards dismay,
They saw the three were not afraid—
And not just three, but counted four—
One they'd never seen before!

---

[164] Dan. 3:17–18

God's angel stood and walked with them,
And not an ember touched their hem!
Because the king's erected statue
Was built without good virtue.
God's mighty hand protected them
To show the royal diadem,
Is not crowned on earthly kings,
But rightfully crowned on the King of Kings![165]

---

[165] stanza 2; Dan. 3:1–30

TURNING AROUND
Hosea

"I will show love to the one I called 'not my loved one'. I will say to those called 'not my people', you are my people', and they will say, 'you are my God'" (Hosea 2:23).

For all the ones with hurting hearts,
Grasping for a brand-new start.
For all the ones who've been told,
And then again retold;
You're not quite enough,
Or thought you're unloved.

The deception that stained,
No words can explain.
No place to go where you belong—
An inner struggle for so long.
Things you felt all by yourself,
Thoughts that never cleared the shelf.[166]

Neglected, rejected,
Alone and subjected.
All that shut the door on love,
God can open in His love.
What Satan tried to steal,
God alone can heal.[167]

---

[166] stanza 1 and 2; Hos. 1:6–2:1
[167] stanza 3; Hos. 9:8; 14:8; 2:6, 7; 11:1

In the midst of all the strife,
It's God who gives new life.
In loving care, He will surround
And bind up all your open wounds.
Through His gracious, open door,
By His love He will restore.[168]

From the dark and slippery slope,
To the promise of His hope.
The Lord will be your healing balm,
His peace will be your inner calm.
To life in him where you belong,
Forever now and all life long! [169]

---

[168] stanza 4; Hos. 10:12; 14:4
[169] stanza 5; Hos. 2:15; 2:19; 12:6

LOCUS CALLED
Joel

"The Lord says, 'I will give you back what you lost to the swarming locus'" (Joel 2:25).

"The sun will be turned to darkness and the moon to blood before the coming of the great and dreadful day of The Lord. But everyone who calls on the name of The Lord will be saved" (Joel 2:31–32).

"Everyone who calls upon the name of The Lord will be saved" (Joel 2:32).

Part 1

Faith stumbled,
Honor crumbled.
Truth perverted,
Then deserted.
Sin gripped,
Footing slipped.
From seduction,
Led destruction.
Love affair'ed,
Stripped bare.
Lions devoured
And overpowered.
Peace captured,
Forsaken pasture.
Faithless hooks,
Dried brooks.

Hunger gripped,
Spiritually stripped.
Flocks abandoned,
Shepherds absconded.
Marked rapine,
Extent unseen.
Locus swarmed
In reform.[170]

Part 2

Oh, hear,
Give ear!
The Lord,
They ignored!
At times,
We've declined,
And ignored
His restore.
Judgment blurred,
Path deterred.
They wandered
And squandered.
Then stumbled—
Strength crumbled.
Shadows ensnared.
Wisdom, impaired.
Sin flirted.
Truth everted.
Deception sparked,
Leaving parched.[171]

---

[170] stanza 1; Joel 1:1–15; 3:19; 1:20
[171] stanza 2; Joel 2:1; 1:14, 15

Part 3

Your Word
Be heard!
The Lord
Restores!
Truth reputes,
Heart's dispute.
Locus strips
Sin's grip,
Prayers rise
At demise.
Sin spurned
Heart's return!
God restore,
Us before!
True light,
Will ignite!
Making broader,
Living water.
The Shepherd's,
Promised pasture.
Exalted High,
We glorify.
Holy one,
Salvation rung!
Zion bound,
Heaven crowned![172]

---

[172] stanza 3; Joel 2:25; 3:9, 10; 2:27; 3:18; 2:10; 3:14; 2:12–3:21

TRUE MEASURE
Amos

"This is what he showed me: The Lord was standing by a wall that had been built true to plumb, with a plumb line in His hand. And The Lord asked me, 'what do you see Amos'? 'A plumb line' I replied" (Amos 7:7–8).

"But let justice roll on like a river, and righteousness like a never-failing stream" (Amos 5:24)

Amos saw a vision,
A display of God's precision.
The Lord stood by a temple wall,
Bricks of generations tall.[173]

Inspection proved how pure the line.
A plumb line's tool of truth aligned.
A testing of the heart's estate,
To show cracks of deviate.[174]

Oh, test the heart and realign,
With God's single, pure design!
Do what's right and run from evil,
Don't get lost in the upheaval.[175]

---

[173] stanza 1; Amos 1:1; 7:7
[174] stanza 2; Amos 7:8, 9; "The Plumbline" Spurgeon's Sermon Notes, Charles H. Spurgeon, 1997, Hendrickson Publishers, Inc.
[175] stanza 3; Amos 5:14, 15

For His righteous vindication,
Is to the temple's reformation.
It's promised in His restoration
By His holy separation.[176]

From the ruins, He'll rebuild.
His glory ever be fulfilled.
The righteous, held in Him upright,
Standing in His glorious light.[177]

Together joined to lift His praise,
United strong, His wall is raised.
In His name, as we proclaim,
The Lord of heaven is His name![178]

Let justice roll on like a river,
For the Lord, our God, delivers!
Let righteousness be a flowing stream,
For the righteous one will come redeem![179]
And living hope, a refreshing spring—
A gift His living water brings!

---

[176] stanza 4; Amos 5:1–12; 3:3
[177] stanza 5; Amos 9:9–11
[178] stanza 7; Amos 4:13
[179] stanza 8; Amos 5:24

PRIDEFUL DECEIT
Obadiah

"The pride of your heart has deceived you, you who live in the clefts of the rocks and make your home on the heights, who say to yourself, 'who can bring me to the ground?' Though you soar like the eagle and make your nest amount the stars, from there I will cut you down" (Obadiah 1:3–4).

Lessons from Edom,
Where evil clung.[180]
God forewarned,
But people scorned.
For love departed,
From calloused hearts[181]
And egotism,
Refused to listen[182]
Or even petition,
Lest be forgiven.[183]
Deceived by pride,
Pushed God aside.[184]
Arrogance swelled
In evil's rebel.
Mouths that boast,
With nothing to toast.[185]

---

[180] Ob verses 1–7
[181] 13
[182] 14
[183] 11
[184] 3
[185] 4

Scoffing at others suffering,
Revealed the hearts uncovering.[186]
Stumbling in self-reside
Instead of in the lion's pride,[187]
For one's own glory crashes down,
But ever is the Lord's renown![188]
In the end, He remains,
The Lord our God forever reigns![189]

---

[186] 12
[187] 15, 16
[188] 17
[189] 20, 21

THE RELUCTANT PROPHET
—————— Jonah ——————

"The Lord replied, 'Is it right for you to be angry about this?'" (Jonah 4:4).

God said, "Go to Nineveh,"
But Jonah felt hysteria.
Thinking they would have him killed,
Anger's wrath toward them spilled.
By impulse Jonah chose,
God's good will to oppose.
Gripped in fear's objection,
He ran the opposite direction.
But boarding a ship
Was still in God's script.
Heaven's winds rained down attention
On the prophet's wayward contention,
Even so, he willed to drown,
Before he was willing to turn around.
But escaping God was no avail,
When swallowed by a whale.[190]

Excuses began to glare,
In the confines of solitaire.
In the dark of those three days,
Jonah chose to then obey.
Humbled in prayer,
God's praises declared.

---

[190] stanza1; Jonah 1:1–17

By God's command,
He was brought to land.
And Jonah spoke God's message,
To the city of godless wreckage.
The people repented
And God relented,
Forgiving the sin,
When they sought within.[191]

But Jonah's pride set in
And anger swelled therein;
He wanted to be right,
Even though it wasn't right.
As someone once said,[192]
Of hearts misled:

"We are God's chosen few,
All others will be dammed.
There is no place in heaven for you,
We can't have heaven crammed"[193]
(Jonathan Swift).

Though Jonah proved obedient,
He missed the main ingredient:
But dare we compare,
Just to be fair ...
Who's turned in fear,
Although sincere?
Or harbored hate,
And trusted fate?

---

[191] stanza 2; Jonah 2:1–10; 3:3–10
[192] stanza 3; Jonah 4:1–11
[193] Jonah Literature Network, 1731, *The Poems of Jonathan Swift*, "The Place of The Damned"

Afraid the truth would take a toll,
Instead of serving in your role.
What a tragedy to quit,
Instead of to the Lord commit!
May we seek deliverance
And leave behind indifference.

Don't hide beneath the deck,
When storms forewarn a wreck.
Wake up, oh, sleeping Christian,
And choose your disposition.
Be humbled by sin,
And His patience within.
Do not seclude and isolate,
But share God's love for He is great!
For His name's sake,
Keep your heart and soul awake!
With gratitude and humble heart,
Display the mercy love imparts.

NO GRAY LINES
Micah

"But as for me, I watch in hope for The Lord, I wait for God my Savior, my God will hear me. Do not gloat over me my enemy! Though I have fallen, I will rise. Though I sit in darkness, The Lord will be my light. Because I have sinned against Him, I will bear The Lord's wrath, until he pleads my case and upholds my cause. He will bring me out into the light; I will see His righteousness" (Micah 7:7–9).

The naysayers doubt,
Few dare think about.
Deafening an ear to judgment
Will not stop the sounding trumpet.
Evil will turn and hide its face,
Shamed in all its lowly disgrace.
Micah declared,
Doom and despair
On haters of good,
Where blasphemy stood.
Darkened by evil,
Deceived in upheaval.
Sin bred abound,
Where no light was found.
The prophets' cry,
Beckoned on high.
To turn and seek God's way
Before the coming of the day.
For hope remains,
In the Lord's domain.

From God above,
In unfailing love.[194]
His holy name,
The saints proclaim.
Seek mercy's light
And do what's right.
For He redeems,
And intervenes.
The Father God Creator,
In mercy's grace is greater;
His grace is greater
Than all our failures.
And grace is greater
Than sinful behavior.
In blessed hope,
From grace that flows.
To the eyes of faith that see,
And hearts that bow on bended knee—
He hurls sin into the ocean,
In perfect show of love's devotion.
A faithfulness of love bestowed,
As He promised long ago.
God's Word will stand forever,
Forever and ever. Amen![195]

---

[194] stanza 1; Mic. 2:6, 7; 1:2–6; 2:10; 2:1–5; 3:6–8; 1:8; 7:16, 17; 7:7
[195] stanza 2; Mic. 2:12, 13; 6:8; 7:8–10; 7:15–20

HE BECKONS
Nahum

"The Lord is good, a refuge in time of trouble. He cares for those who trust in Him, but with an overwhelming flood He will make an end to Nineveh; He will pursue His foes into the realm of darkness. Whatever they plot against The Lord, He will bring to an end" (Nahum 1:7–9).

Heaven breathed compassion
Within the heart of Nahum.
His breath was for the people,
Whose faith, at best, was feeble.
Though their downfall was foretold,
Eternal hope, he then retold.[196]

In warning after warning,
Came an outcry for reforming.
For in the day of trouble,
Earthly things will turn to rubble.
When all else has been stripped away,
Choose to cling and then obey.[197]

And when the eye cannot discern,
Trust evil's time will crash and burn.
Beyond the seen that seems unclear,
Our heavenly Father has declared:
His faithful promise is secure,
Through time and space it will endure.[198]

---

[196] stanza 1; Nah. 1:1
[197] stanza 2; Nah. 1:3–6
[198] stanza 3; Nah. 2:2

He will surely come and rescue
And provide a place of refuge.
His stronghold's always strong
And beckons where the heart belongs.
Here on earth or up in heaven,
Hope is found in His redemption.[199]

By faith, no matter great or small,
In that day, not one will fall.
Not even one will be condemned
Of the hearts that trust in Him.
The Father knows all His by name,
Each one of who, His name proclaims.[200]

---

[199] stanza 4; Nah. 7:7
[200] stanza 5; Nah. 1:7

LIVING FAITH
Habakkuk

"I will stand at my watch and station myself on the ramparts; I will look to see what He will say to me, and what answer I am going to give to this complaint. Then The Lord replied: Write down the revelation and make it plain on tablets so that a herald may run with it. For the revelation awaits an appointed time; it speaks of the end and it will not prove false. Though it linger, wait for it; it will certainly come and will not delay" (Habakkuk 2:1–3)

Of the minor's, he's the eighth.
And his name means "to embrace"
And embrace he did,
In the storms amid.
Habakkuk knew,
What few pursue—[201]

He believed by faith,
Not in faith of *faith*
By power in God, a living faith,
In the presence of His holy place.
For God will not bend His will to our whim,
But instead He will show the way to Him.[202]

---

[201] stanza 1; Hab. 2:1
[202] stanza 2; Hab. 2:4; 2:14; 2:20

When what God said did not seem right,
The prophet did not feel contrite.
Instead he asked the reason why,
In humble stance to clarify.
He sought to know more clearly
And embraced God's will sincerely.[203]

When the visions laid before
Were promised doom of pending war,
Where the vine would be stripped bare,
And nothing would be left to spare.
No flock left in the fold,
But still, his words to God extolled.[204]

In the face of despair,
He bowed in prayer.
He responded not in hesitation
But sung of joy in God's salvation.
Humbled by the remaining mystery,
Marked his faith in claiming victory.[205]

For God will answer and fortify,
The reverent heart that's unified.
He knew the Lord someday'd restore,
Proclaiming strength within the Lord.
For those within the Lord remain
Sustained by what His plan ordains.[206]

---

[203] stanza 3; Hab. 2:1; 1:1–3; 1:12, 13; 3:8
[204] stanza 4; Hab. 2:9–17; 3:1
[205] stanza 5; Hab. 3:18, 19; 3:2
[206] stanza 6; Hab. 3:17–19

HEART'S CONDITION
Zephaniah

"She obeys no one, she accepts no correction. She does not draw near to her God" (Zephaniah 3:2).

"Morning by morning He dispenses His justice, and every new day He does not fail, yet the unrighteous know no shame" (Zephaniah 3:5).

"Do not fear Zion; do not let your hands go limp. The Lord your God is with you, The Mighty Warrior who saves. He will take great delight in you; in His love He will no longer rebuke you, but will rejoice over you with singing" (Zephaniah 3:16–17).

Zephaniah's plea heeds inquisition,
To search into the heart's condition.
Past the blatant outright sin,
A search to see what's deep within.
Longer than a glance might show,
Of sins not counted or to know.
For the sins of commission
And weight of omission.[207]

Oh, turn from all unrighteousness,
Examine heedless blitheful-ness.
Loose the grasp of godless idols
And lean into a holy revival.

---

[207] stanza 1; Zeph. 1:4–7

Or God Himself will rid the grasp
In furry that causes angels to gasp.
The day of the Lord is near at hand,
A day through the ages that's been planned.[208]

His day of reckon will consume,
And in this day, a day of doom.
Woe to the rebellious,
Whose heart's refused to trust,
To obey the Lord or learn correction
And fought against in willful rejection.
For God will bring justice to the light,
In a holy fire He will ignite.[209]

But those who serve Him will remain,
By His love in Him sustained.
Divine in judgment's purity,
With His light He'll purify.
His judgment brings deliverance,
To those who give Him reverence.
For God is faithful, forgiving sin,
To all who come and enter in.[210]

The Lord delights in true repentance.
Rejoicing in those who seek His presence,
It is our hope of future blessing,
In the coming day of His descending.
To God give praise and glorify
He'll cleanse our hearts and purify,
Acceptable to give Him praise,
Where we'll forever be amazed![211]

---

[208] stanza 2; Zeph. 2:10
[209] stanza 3; Zeph. 3:8
[210] stanza 4; Zeph. 3:9–11
[211] stanza 5; Zeph. 2:4;2:14; 3:8; 3:18, 19

YOUR TREASURE
Haggai

"This is what The Lord almighty says: 'Give careful thought to your ways. Go up into the mountains and bring down timber and build my house, so that I may take pleasure in it and be honored,' says The Lord. You expected so much, but see, it turned out to be little. What you brought home, I blew away. Why?' declares The Lord Almighty. 'Because of you the heavens have withheld their dew and the earth its crops" (Haggai 1:7–10).

Are your treasures hidden in hereby,
Or do they shine in heaven's high?
Are they raised in glory for the Lord
Or to be cut down by the sword?[212]

The time is now, not down the road,
Before intent starts to erode.
He bids to purge, atone and cleanse,
Not through our lens but by His holy, spotless lens.[213]

To God lift up a sacrifice,
To the one who paid our price—
For this brings honor to the Lord,
And His pleasure's our reward.[214]

---

[212] stanza 1; Hag. 1:4–6
[213] stanza 2: Hag. 1:8–10; 2:14
[214] stanza 3; Hag. 2:4

He blesses when we heed His call,
A bond in Him that will not fall.
Today, tomorrow and ever true,
His promise holds to be with you.[215]

He gives to us His Holy Spirit,
A covenant that faith inherits.
The bond God promised is Himself,
In heart and soul to always dwell.[216]

He spoke ahead of greater glory,
Where sacrifice crowned King of glory.
In the greatest ever sacrifice,
The wondrous sacrifice of Christ![217]

---

[215] stanza 4; Hag. 1:13
[216] stanza 5; Hag. 2:5
[217] stanza 6; Hag. 2:19; John 3:16

GOD'S LOVE LETTER
Zechariah

"Then I myself, will be a protective wall of fire around Jerusalem, says The Lord. And I will be the glory inside the city" (Zechariah 2:5).

"Who dares despise the day of small things, since the seven eyes of The Lord that range throughout the earth will rejoice when they see the chosen capstone" (Zechariah 4:10).

"My love for Mount Zion is passionate and strong; I am consumed with passion for Jerusalem! And now The Lord says: I am returning to Mt Zion, and I will live in Jerusalem. Then Jerusalem will be called the faithful city" (Zechariah 8:2–3).

"All this may seem impossible to you now, a small remnant of God's people. But is it impossible for me? says The Lord of Heaven's Armies. This is what The Lord of Heaven's Armies says: You can be sure that I will rescue my people from the East and from the West" (Zechariah 8:6–7).

Return to me, and I will return to you,
For I am your God, faithful and true.
I have heard your cries,
And I sympathize.
I will comfort you in mercy,
So turn to me and cease to worry.
My love is strong and it will not fade.
I Am your God so do not be afraid.[218]

---

[218] stanza 1; Zech. 1:3; 8:8; 10:6; 1:13; 8:13

For I have chosen you,
And I will see you through.
I will rescue you,
And my hand will protect you.
My glory is a fortifier,
Surrounded by a wall of fire-
There you will be free and safe,
When you enter in my holy place.[219]

For this is where I'll live with you,
Where my holy love pursues,
Always present, burning strong,
Consuming love, eternal long.
You're my precious possession,
For whom I hold affection.
I've washed away the dirt and blight,
And clothed you in a radiant white.[220]

I've rejected Satan's accusations,
And redeemed you from his allegations.
Do not be discouraged taking small steps,
Faith will shine by efforts reflect
And I rejoice to see you begin.
A new beginning from where you've been.
Be strong my child, keep taking steps.
I will be with you through the depths.[221]

---

[219] stanza 2; Zech. 3:2; 9:15, 16; 2:5; 9:11
[220] stanza 3; Zech. 2:10; 8:2; 2:8
[221] stanza 4; Zech. 3:2; 10:8; 4:10; 8:6; 8:9

FIERCE LOVE
Malachi

"Then those who feared The Lord spoke with each other and The Lord listened to what they said. In His presence, a scroll of remembrance was written to record the names of those who feared Him and always thought about the honor of His name. 'They will be my people', says The Lord of Heaven's Armies. 'On the day when I act in judgment, they will be my own special treasure. I will spare them as a father spares an obedient child. Then you again will see the difference between the righteous and the wicked, between those who serve God and those who do not'" (Malachi 3:17).

The Lord has been and stood before,
A love by which can't be ignored.
His word revealed the light of truth,
To which it offers no dispute.
He's marked us as His own possession,
In His love's jealous ignition.
For we are indeed, His special treasure.
His love has proved beyond all measure.[222]

May we never offer less than worthy,
And hope to risk His hand of mercy.
May we not defile His holy table,
Lest consequence be ever fatal.

---

[222] stanza 1; Mal. 1:2; 1:5; 3:3, 4; 3:17

May we never lose a servant's heart,
Lest His holy Word depart.
The Lord's fierce love will come against,
The day His power is dispensed.[223]

If contempt should steal our heart's devotion,
May He lay us first to dust's erosion,
And send us early to the grave
Before the day our heart's betray.
May we ever lift His holy name,
In life and death, His name proclaim.
In action, word, and deed,
His Word to always heed.[224]

And keep in heart and mind and soul,
His faithful love to Him extol.
Though both at times we're sinner and saint—
You are the Lord who will not change!
Keep us in Your light, we pray,
Help us to obey each day.
Fight for us in Your great love,
Protect us for You up above.[225]

---

[223] stanza 2; Mal. 1:10–12; 2:6; 4:1
[224] stanza 3; Mal. 2:2; 3:7; 2:5, 6; 4:4
[225] stanza 4; Mal. 3:6; 4:2, 3

AFTERWORD

Reading the Bible is a lengthy, worthwhile process, one that every Christian should commit to at the right time. *Hope through the Ages* offers a unique way of familiarizing the reader with the scriptures and people of the Old Testament as a starting point. It is also a refresher in the lifelong journey of our daily walk with the Lord.

ABBREVIATIONS

BOOKS OF THE BIBLE

OLD TESTAMENT

Genesis	Gen.
Exodus	Ex.
Leviticus	Lev.
Numbers	Num.
Deuteronomy	Deut.
Joshua	Josh.
Judges	Judg.
Ruth	Ruth
1 Samuel	1 Sam.
2 Samuel	2 Sam.
1 Kings	1 Kings
2 Kings	2 Kings
1 Chronicles	1 Chron.
2 Chronicles	2 Chron.
Ezra	Ezra
Nehemiah	Neh.
Esther	Est.
Job	Job
Psalms	Ps.
Proverbs	Prov.
Ecclesiastes	Eccl.
Song of Songs	Song
Isaiah	Isa.
Jeremiah	Jer.
Lamentations	Lam.
Ezekiel	Ezek.
Daniel	Dan.
Hosea	Hos.
Joel	Joel
Amos	Amos
Obadiah	Obad.
Jonah	Jonah
Micah	Mic.
Nahum	Nah.
Habakkuk	Hab.
Zephaniah	Zeph.
Haggai	Hag.
Zechariah	Zech.
Malachi	Mal.

NEW TESTAMENT REFERENCES

Matthew	Matt.
John	John
Romans	Rom.
Hebrews	Heb.
Galatians	Gal.
Revelations	Rev.